THE ADVENTURES OF COWGIRL AMY!

Cowgirl Amy
and
Favorite Prayers
for Mom

Dr. Psalm

The Adventures of Cowgirl Amy!
Cowgirl Amy and Favorite Prayers for Mom by Dr. Psalm
Copyright © 2014 by Peace Psalm LLC
All Rights Reserved.
ISBN: 978-1-59755-369-8

Published by: ADVANTAGE BOOKS™
    Longwood, Florida USA
    www.advbookstore.com

This book and parts thereof may not be reproduced in any form, stored in a retrieval system or transmitted in any form by any means (electronic, mechanical, photocopy, recording or otherwise) without prior written permission of the author, except as provided by United States of America copyright law.

First Printing: aUGUST 2014
14 15 16 17 18 19 20 10 9 8 7 6 5 4 3 2 1
Printed in the United States of America

Cowgirl Amy and Favorite Prayers for Mom

Dr. Psalm

"Halo and Howdy! My name is Cowgirl Amy! I love God, my family, friends, and my pony Slow Poke!

My Grandma Linda and I go on secret missions. We find God and praise in the most amazing places. Come and join us!

Today I am calling Grandma Linda to help me with special prayers for my mom. She is a wonderful mom, and I want to do something special for her.

Grandma Linda called me today on Skype. I wear my yellow hat when I need her help.

"Halo my Cowgirl Amy! How are you?" asked Grandma.

"I am fine. I need your help doing something special for mom, because she is a wonderful mom!" I said.

Grandma Linda asked "How about a prayer book?"

I said "Alright and Yee Haw! Let's get started!"

Grandma Linda said "Giving thanks to God is always a good thing to do. How about some different ways to say thank you for your mom?"

I said "I know! How about a thank you prayer?"

"Great idea Cowgirl Amy!" said Grandma Linda.

"Let's pray." said Grandma Linda. "And, I will write it in mom's prayer book!" I said!

Dear Heavenly Father, thank you for giving a great mom to me.

I love her, and thank you for making her my mama mom.

In the name of Jesus we pray, Amen!

"What else shall we put in your mom's prayer book?" asked Grandma Linda.

"I know! My mom makes me laugh. She sings funny songs to me until I giggle. I am thankful for a fun mom." I said.

"Sounds like another great prayer to me!" said Grandma Linda as she giggled with me.

"Yee haw! Yes, I am adding smiley faces to this prayer!" I said.

"Excellent ideas Cowgirl Amy! Let's pray and keep writing!" said Grandma Linda. "Yee haw!" I said.

Cowgirl Amy and Favorite Prayers for Mom

Dear Lord, thank you for a nice mom, who takes time to sing to me and make me laugh.

Thank you for a nice mom, who walks with me down Your path.

In the name of Jesus we pray, Amen!

"You have a lot of great things to thank God for your mom. What is next Cowgirl Amy?" asked Grandma Linda.

"Reading the Bible! My mom reads the Bible to me. This makes me happy!" I said.

"It sounds like another prayer is in order." said Grandma Linda as she smiled at me.

"My pen is ready to go!" I said!

Dear Heavenly Father, thank you for a mom, who reads the Bible to me.

Thank you for a mom, who teaches and lives the Christian faith.

In the name of Jesus we pray, Amen!

"Does your mom have a favorite color?" asked Grandma Linda?

"Yes, she likes green!" I said.

"How about writing this prayer with a green marker?" asked Grandma Linda.

"Great idea Grandma Linda! I am going to add a cross with love and hearts too!" I said and then giggled. I like giving thanks for my mom.

Cowgirl Amy and Favorite Prayers for Mom

Dear Lord, thank you for my mom.

Thank you for the color green.

Thank you for a mom who loves me and You.

In the name of Jesus we pray, Amen!

"What else shall we put in your mom's prayer book?" asked Grandma Linda.

"I know! Hugs! I am thankful that my mom loves me and hugs me. She is kind and takes care of me. I love my mom." I said.

"Excellent ideas Cowgirl Amy! Let's pray and keep writing in your mom's prayer book!" said Grandma Linda.

"Yee haw!" I said.

Dear Lord, thank you for a great mom, who loves me and hugs me.

Thank you for a mom, who is kind and takes care of me.

In the name of Jesus we pray, Amen!

"I am so glad God blessed you with a wonderful mom." said Grandma Linda.

"Me too! I want to add one more prayer! My mom likes flowers." I said.

"Great idea Cowgirl Amy!" said Grandma Linda.

I am going to add flowers and hearts too!" I said and then giggled.

Cowgirl Amy and Favorite Prayers for Mom

Dear Lord, thank you for my mom.

Thank you for flowers.

Thank you for a mom, who plays Bible Prayer Showers.

In the name of Jesus we pray, Amen!

(See the end of book for a description of the Bible Prayer Shower game.)

Dr. Psalm

Adios for now my friend! Slow Poke and I have a *Favorite Prayers for Mom* book to deliver!

Come and visit us next time when we make a *Favorite Prayers for Dad* book!

Until we meet again! Your friend, Cowgirl Amy

Dear Lord, thank you for my friends, and thank you for all of our moms.

Please watch over them and shower them with your love.

In the name of Jesus we pray, Amen!

Dr. Psalm

Bible Prayer Showers

Bible Prayer Showers is a little game my Grandma Linda made up for me.

Put Bible prayers in a container, and then dump them out from as high as your mom, dad, grandparent, or grown-up friend can reach. Then read the prayers one by one together, and put them back into the jar once you read them.

If you have more than one cowgirl or cowboy, then make sure everyone has a prayer! ☺

Say the Lord's Prayer Together when you are done opening, reading and putting your prayers back for next time.

Prayer Books

You may make your prayer book for your mom out of any material or use the next few pages to write them. The thing that really matters is that the prayers come from your heart.

If you would like to use a prayer book like Cowgirl Amy, they are available on CowgirlAmy.com. It will come blank for you to fill in your favorite prayers for your mom!

My Prayers for Mom

My Prayers for Mom

Join Cowgirl Amy this year in her adventures!

- Cowgirl Amy and the Prayer Garden: A Flower a Day
- Cowgirl Amy and the Easter Adventure – A Tradition Begins
- Cowgirl Amy and Favorite Prayers for Mom
- Cowgirl Amy and Favorite Prayers for Dad
- Cowgirl Amy and the Adventure at the CowKid Zoo
- Cowgirl Amy and the Christmas Celebration – A Tradition Begins

Prayers, blessing and cheer!

For more information contact:

Dr. Psalm
C/O Advantage Books
P.O. Box 160847
Altamonte Springs, FL 32716
info@ advbooks.com

To purchase additional copies of this book or other books published by Advantage Books call our order number at:
407-788-3110 (Book Orders Only)

or visit our bookstore website at: www.advbookstore.com

Longwood, Florida, USA
"we bring dreams to life" ™
www.advbooks.com

www.ingramcontent.com/pod-product-compliance
Lightning Source LLC
Chambersburg PA
CBHW070756050426
42449CB00010B/2495